DANGEROUS
CANDY

DANGEROUS CANDY

A true drug story,
by someone who did them
and kicked them

RAFFAELLA FLETCHER
PETER MAYLE

SINCLAIR-STEVENSON

First published in Great Britain by
Sinclair-Stevenson Limited
7/8 Kendrick Mews
London SW7 3HG, England

British Library Cataloguing in Publication Data

Fletcher, Raffaella
Dangerous candy.
1. Drug addiction – Biographies
I. Title   II. Mayle, Peter
362.293092

ISBN 1-85619-020-X

Photoset by Rowland Phototypesetting Limited
Bury St Edmunds, Suffolk
Printed and bound in Great Britain by
Richard Clay Limited, Bungay, Suffolk

This book is dedicated to

My parents, who from near and far never gave up their belief in me.

All those who were not so fortunate, such as: Craig, François, Hakki.

All those whose destinies I do not know but for whom I hope, such as; Brahms, Francis, Ian, Timothy.

All those who help us to choose to live.

ACKNOWLEDGEMENTS

Acknowledgements are due to a great many people. They all know who they are, and I gratefully thank them from the bottom of my heart.

1

'A NICE, NORMAL GIRL'

I smell clean now, and it's been five years since I stuck a needle in my arm.

I used to go for weeks without taking a bath. I never noticed. Being in filthy clothes didn't matter. Friends didn't matter. I stole and I lied, and that didn't matter. All I thought about was drugs, and getting the money to buy drugs.

I can't remember everything I took, but I do remember these:

There was grass and hash and hash oil, Dalmane, Mogadon, Normison, Xanax, Librium, Valium, Ativan, Tuinal, Nembutal, Seconal, Equanil, Heminevrin, Mandrax, amphetamine sulphate, black bombers, DF 118, Diconal, Temgesic, Methadone, morphine, opium, glue, LSD, STP, magic mushrooms, adrenalin, cocaine and heroin – sometimes on their own, sometimes mixed, often with alcohol. There were others, lots of others, but I was in no state to tell what they were. I tried just about everything except crack, and that was only because crack didn't exist in those days.

That's my drug history in a paragraph, what I used to do every day that I can remember from the age of twelve until I was twenty-four. I was high when I went through school, and I was stoned when I went through a marriage. Somebody once described drugs as the biggest love affair of your life, and that's exactly what it was for me. I thought about nothing else, and there was nothing I wouldn't do for a fix.

I hope it's over, although they say there's no guaranteed cure. But I've stopped eating pills or cooking heroin or sucking LSD. I have a job, and straight friends. Some of them don't know that I spent twelve years on drugs, and sometimes I find it hard to imagine that's how I used to live. It seems far away, and yet it seems like yesterday. It's easier to think it was someone else, and I suppose in a way it was. She was the junkie, and I'm what's left. I lost twelve years of my life, but I could have lost it all, so I'm lucky.

Outside people – straight people – believe that if you look hard enough you can always find The Problem that explains why anyone should get into drugs as deeply as I did, some personal misery that makes real life impossible to cope with. That's the only way they can understand drugs, as an escape from unhappiness – from a broken home, from parents who are drunks, from

2

having no money and no future, from being ugly or lonely or depressed or unloved.

Often, it's not like that at all. It wasn't with me. I didn't have any of those excuses. My parents were happy together, and still are. They loved me, and gave me everything I could need: their affection, their time, their interest, a room of my own, nice clothes, pocket money. I was their only child and they probably spoiled me, but not too much. I was a lucky middle-class kid in a happy middle-class home.

I wasn't a genius, but I certainly wasn't a dunce. I had no trouble getting into a decent school, and I didn't find the lessons hard. I got on well with teachers and the other kids. I wasn't overweight or cross-eyed or freaky looking. I didn't have a stammer or a limp or any kind of physical handicap that could have made me feel different from anyone else. I looked older than my age, but that didn't really bother me. I was shy and awkward, like most girls of eleven, but people seemed to like me. Nobody could have looked at me and seen The Problem. There was no reason why I shouldn't have grown up with anything more serious to worry about than boyfriends and pimples.

And yet, with no excuses and no need to escape from anything, I still got myself into a mess that almost killed me. Now that I've met hundreds of other addicts, I know that I wasn't the only one to come from a normal, comfortable background and slip into a dirty and frightening world.

Addiction is a disease, and like all diseases, it can infect anybody. You're just as likely to find a coke-head or a smack jockey in Belgravia as in Brixton. If you have the disease, all it takes is a little money, a little freedom, a little curiosity, and before you know it you're starting to look for the people with the powder and the pills. And they're never far away. Even then, they were never far away.

There is no single reason that accounts for the first experiments which lead to addiction. I've heard people put it down to pressure from friends, the need to feel grown-up and sharp and cool, the search to find something more exciting than getting on a bus and going to school or work. I've heard about models doing drugs to lose weight (just for a week or two, they always say, just so I look good for the job). I've met people who started because they couldn't get to sleep, or they couldn't stay awake. Because they had too much work, or because they couldn't find a job. Because they were scared of flying or dying or failing. There are hundreds of excuses.

With me, eleven years old and too young to know much about anything, it was just curiosity. That's all. I wasn't depressed or lonely. Nobody twisted my arm. The whole thing, at least at the beginning, was my choice. Later on, I didn't have a choice.

Like any eleven year old who watches TV and listens to pop music, I was aware that things called drugs existed, and that they did something special. In the early 70s there were plenty of song lyrics about getting kicks from some secret, grown-up treat. And there were TV programmes that mentioned drugs too. They were always careful to make the point that drugs were forbidden.

What were drugs? What were kicks? I didn't know, but they sounded interesting, and being forbidden made them more interesting. I should have asked my parents about them, but I didn't. I didn't want to, because I thought I knew what their answer would be. Even then, I was sly. All addicts are.

I talked to my friends at school, but they didn't know any more than I did, and most of them didn't want to. That should have been enough to make me lose interest too, but instead it did exactly the opposite. I grew more and more determined to find out what kicks were all about.

It would be easier today. I know there are schools in London – even good, expensive schools – where some of the pupils are small-time dealers. That hadn't happened yet in my school, and anyway I didn't know what to ask for. So I decided that if I couldn't buy drugs, I'd have to make them myself.

The only drug name I knew was grass, and there was no shortage of grass in the London parks – piles of it, everywhere. I couldn't understand why more people weren't collecting it if it made you feel so good. When I got home and tried to smoke it, I understood. Wrong grass. No kicks.

I had a vague idea that drugs might be herbs or spices. Then someone told me you could get high on nutmeg, so I raided the kitchen and found some. It smelt strong and strange, like I imagined drugs ought to smell. But were you supposed to sniff it, or smoke it, or suck it? I tried them all and made myself sick. I tried incense. All that gave me was a headache. My final experiment in home-made drugs was banana skins soaked in brandy and then dried. I didn't even get a headache from them. Nothing.

If I'd been normal, it would probably have ended there, with just a rotten taste in my mouth. But I knew I hadn't found whatever it was that made people talk about turning on and getting high, and I couldn't leave it alone. I know now, although I didn't then, that I have an addict's personality. I can't dip my toe in the water. I have to jump in.

My curiosity about drugs took over, and nagged away at me every day. I *had* to try a real drug, just to see what it was like. At an age when most girls are dreaming about rockstars or ponies, I was dreaming about getting high. I was hooked on the idea of drugs.

The rest was only a matter of time.

2

STARTING

My first period came when I was eleven. It made me more shy, more awkward, more confused. I felt as if I was someone small walking around in a body several sizes too big. That's nothing unusual. Most girls go through it and get over it without diving into grass and alcohol and chemicals. But I thought it was worse for me – it had to be worse for me because I was different and special. In fact, what I was developing along with breasts and the other normal signs of growing up was an ego as big as a house.

My problems were heavier than other people's problems. My happiness was more important. I was more important. It was all part of my classic addict's equipment. I was addicted to me.

More and more, I began to feel that drugs were not just interesting and exciting, but if I could only get my hands on some they might take away the shyness, get rid of the confusion in my head, put everything right, make life fun. Other people looked as though they were having fun, and I wanted what they had. This was going to happen again, much later, in a very different way – the feeling of having my nose pressed up against a window, looking at something better and wanting it, my classic, self-centred view of the world.

I went with some friends to a Rolling Stones concert. We didn't have tickets, but tickets were only needed at the front. We broke in at the back, and found ourselves twenty feet from the stage – twenty feet from Mick Jagger and Keith Richards, blasted by the music, blinded by the lights, surrounded by hot bodies, sweating, dancing, friendly bodies. Cans of beer were being passed round, and there was a strange, good smell in the air.

I didn't know the boy I was next to in the crowd, and I never saw him again, but he gave me my first hit. It was a small, soggy sweet-smelling joint. I didn't think twice; I didn't even think once. I just took it. This was a real drug, what I'd been waiting for.

There are plenty of people who don't like to accept a basic fact about drugs. They look at the end result and see misery or death (how many old addicts do you meet?), but they don't think about the beginning, that from the very first hit some drugs make some people feel fantastic. It doesn't always happen, but when it happens to you, you don't forget it. And you want more. Once is never enough.

The joint and the beer and the music did it for me. I wasn't shy or awkward any more. I was relaxed. I floated through the evening. It wasn't a superhuman rush, but it was enough to make me feel that I understood what it was to get high. I loved it. I was twelve.

And if grass could make me feel like this, what would other, stronger drugs make me feel like? Higher, better, more confident. I could change my feelings whenever I wanted to. I could control them, and all the sharp edges of reality would disappear. I couldn't wait to try something else.

My parents took me to dinner at a friend's house, and I met the first in a series of older men who would help me get hooked. He wasn't very old as 'older' men go – only sixteen – but he seemed twice my age. He wasn't impressed when I told him I'd smoked grass. He preferred hash. The high was different, and you could do it at home because it didn't have the giveaway smell of grass. I didn't leave him alone until he promised to let me have some.

He came round to the house and I told my mother we were going to my room to listen to music. I had my first cookery lesson as I watched him prepare the hash and heat it up, trapping the smoke in a glass. In the beginning, I loved to watch drugs being prepared, knowing that something good was coming, enjoying the wait. In the end, all that goes. You can't wait.

The glass turned cloudy, then thick grey. I sucked up the smoke like a greedy baby taking milk, and then everything fell into place. I was calm, life was wonderful, and I lay on the bed feeling as though the inside of my head was being stroked, very gently stroked, not quite awake, not quite asleep. He was right. The high was different.

I started skipping lunch at school, using my lunch money to buy hash or grass, getting high between lessons. I found new friends, drug friends. Once you start using drugs you can pick other users out from a crowd as if they have a sign on their foreheads saying dope. You don't need to worry about whether or not you're going to like them. You know you'll like them. They like drugs. It takes some time before you realise that not all users are friends. But friends don't matter once you're hooked.

I couldn't believe how many drugs there were, or how good they all looked. Every day it seemed that someone would tell me about something I hadn't tried, some bright, pretty pill that would calm me down or cheer me up. I tried downers – barbiturates like Tuinal. I stole Valium and Mogadon from my mother's bedroom drawer, and followed another piece of expert advice by mixing them with alcohol to get a better hit. By the time I was thirteen, I was washing pills down with vodka before going off to school in the mornings. I thought if I added water to the bottle nobody would notice that the level had dropped.

And nobody did. My parents didn't suspect a thing. If I was difficult or moody, they put it down to the normal aches and pains of growing up. All thirteen year olds are sometimes difficult and moody. It wasn't that they didn't care. They simply didn't know what to look for. They couldn't recognise the signs, and to make it harder for them I was turning into a very good liar.

There was always an excuse to explain why I was home late, why I would lock myself in my room, why I was doing badly at school. The truth was that I was bunking off lessons to get high, or to sneak into pubs. Drugs and boys had replaced history and geography. When I look at my school reports now, I can see my progress down the hill described in the teachers' notes.

The first year (not using anything):

'Raffaella tries hard.'
'Raffaella works with great enthusiasm.'
'Raffaella has maintained a consistently high standard.'

The second year (smoking grass and hash):

'Work is erratic.'
'Work is careless.'
'Work is disorganised.'

The third year (grass, hash, pills and vodka):

'She has let herself slide.'
'She attends lessons but does not participate.'

11

'She has made no effort at all.'
'She has lost interest.'
'A sad report.'

There were arguments at home. My parents couldn't understand why I'd started well and gone to pieces. I told them that I was unhappy and nervous and depressed, and that I couldn't concentrate and hated school. For once, that was the truth, but I didn't say it was all because I was popping pills and drinking vodka. When you're stoned it's hard to concentrate on anything, let alone physics.

Like the textbook addict that I was, my instinct when faced with any bad situation was to run away from it, physically and emotionally, and to find a solution somewhere else. Pills weren't making me happy, so I took more, and fed the disease. Home life was a problem, so I spent as much time as I could away from home, using my bedroom window as a secret front door.

As my school education fell apart, my drug education made what the teachers would call satisfactory progress. My professor was a man of twenty-five. I met him at a party, he took me to see a movie and he introduced me to speed.

Another exciting little ritual, this time with a rolled-up banknote and a tiny pile of powder, my first snort. I felt the effect first in my gut, then it spread up through my body, filling it with energy. My head felt clear; I felt on top and powerful and confident. I could handle anything.

Then the effect wore off and I came down and I just felt empty. What else was there to do but have another snort?

Money for drugs was never a problem in those days. I wasn't using anything too expensive, I had a Saturday job in a shop, and there was always the professor with his contacts and his free-trial offers. He didn't force them on me. I was happy to take the little bags he'd make up – the pocket assortment, a weekend kit of downers and speed and hash, everything I needed to make me feel how I wanted to feel, at least for a few minutes or a few hours.

I turned fifteen, and celebrated by doing hash with hot knives, another way of cooking it to make a huge gust of smoke, and a bigger hit. I thought it was a lot more fun than blowing out the candles on a cake. It was the last birthday I have any memories of for quite a few years.

School was taking up too much time. I'm sure the teachers weren't surprised or sad to see me go, but there was more trouble at home. My parents were puzzled and angry. They thought they had a bright daughter who was behaving like an idiot, and they couldn't understand why. They tried being kind, they tried being tough, they sent me to a psychiatrist who said I was mentally disturbed. He was right. Part of me knew that I was hurting myself and my parents, and part of me couldn't care less. But whenever the struggle in my head became too much to cope with, I reached for the pills or the hash or the speed to escape. I'd think about reality later. Another high would help me sort it out.

I got a full-time job, probably the most unlikely person ever to work in a health-food shop. I'd sit there stoned, surrounded by products which offered a cleaner, healthier life, wondering if there was any way to get high on soyabean curd.

There were parties, there were new pills, there were new men. It's been said that addicts change partners as often as straight people have haircuts. Some don't, some do. For them, it's part of running away from reality, another kind of fix. You tell yourself it doesn't really matter. After pumping your body full of chemicals, what harm can a little sex do? And maybe somewhere, if you keep looking, you'll find a man who can give you the answer. The fact that you don't even know what the question is – apart from a vague wail of self-pity, why aren't I happy? – is too hard to deal with. So you use a man the same way you would use some speed. What's the difference? It's all fine if it gives you a rush. Feelings of right and wrong don't come into it. Drugs put them to sleep very early on.

I met a man called Steve. He was Australian, about twenty-eight, a musician, a nice guy, not a junkie. Not yet. He smoked grass, but that was it. I fell in love with him. He would make me happy, and so I had to have him.

My parents were furious, and there were longer, more angry sessions whenever I put in one of my guest appearances at home. I'd

14

dropped out of school, I had a nothing job and now I was running around with a man almost twice my age. What was the matter with me?

I knew the answer to questions like that. When you can't duck and you can't talk your way out of it, you run away. I left home at sixteen and went off with Steve on my geographicals.

For many addicts, geographicals are the third type of fix. If drugs and sex aren't making you happy in London, try drugs and sex in Paris, in Birmingham, in Thailand, in Amsterdam – it doesn't matter where as long as it's not here. Just keep moving and using, and perhaps you can leave the hard part of life behind. Addict's logic: scratch the travel itch and everything will work out.

Steve had some work in Los Angeles, and California sounded like heaven – sunshine, high-grade cocaine and nobody to ask me questions I didn't want to answer. LA was the place where life would all come together, and I'd find happiness under the palm trees. When I told my parents, they were hurt and sad and worried sick, but that was OK, because I was going to be happy. Then I'd write and tell them, and they'd be happy too.

For a while, it was better than London. I worked as a receptionist, Steve worked at his music and there was always enough money to score. And cocaine was less rough, a much better class of hit than speed. For me, it had a bigger rush – more power, more energy, more of that feeling I always wanted of being in control. So I smoked and we snorted and we drifted through a hundred sunny days with the blinds down in half-dark rooms.

My conscience wasn't entirely numb, and I used to write letters to my parents telling them what good, clean fun their runaway daughter was having. I liked letters, because I could take my time to edit the truth, and I didn't have to answer any questions. My parents kept everything I wrote. They believed it all, I suppose because they wanted to believe it. I have some of the letters in front of me now, and they read as though I was permanently visiting Disneyland.

'We stopped at Santa Claus Lane for a hot bagel and a date shake.'

'We had dinner by the side of a big pool which had a seal in it. Fish and chips! We saved some fish and gave it to the seal.'

'Everywhere we go here is food, and I'm having to be really careful!'

'We had margaritas and stingers. Wow!'

'We stopped in this hillbilly bar. It was fun but pretty weird.'

'Don't worry because I'm healthy and well.'

And stoned. But I didn't think I needed to put that in. Anyone reading those letters – anyone who wanted to think the best rather than the worst – would assume that they were written by a normal, slightly dizzy teenager. There's nothing about coke dealers and guns, or the daily highs and the hours spent in a whacked-out trance. None of that. Just happy, bright, untroubled letters. No wonder my parents were fooled.

It didn't last. After nine months, I realised that wherever the secret of life was, it wasn't in Los Angeles. It must be somewhere else. When Steve went home to Australia, I went with him.

I kept up my letter writing, pages of healthy news about aerobics classes and jogging, but nothing about my new discoveries. I had magic mushrooms for the first time – Gold Tops – either cooked or dipped in honey and eaten raw. They were better than hot bagels in Santa Claus Lane. And one evening I was given my first tab of LSD.

It was the same story all over again. Every time I tried a new drug, I loved it. Other people had bad reactions and nightmare trips from LSD. Not me. I should have known that it was like eating too much ice cream – it was bound to make me ill, but I never thought about that. I had what I thought were a few hours of concentrated happiness. I felt as though my mind had been opened up, as though all of me had been opened up. I felt like a flower in the sun. Sensations were sharper, colours were brighter, the boundaries of reality disappeared. I didn't have to talk, or think. I just felt.

But reality always came back, and I didn't know how to handle reality. I was drifting from high to high in an aimless, vaguely unhappy fog, working at mindless jobs, living with someone I loved and wondering why there was still a great hole

17

in my life. My eighteenth birthday came and went in a blur of extra-strong Thai dope, and when I came out of it there was more trouble with reality. My visa had expired and I was going to have to leave Australia.

I didn't want to leave Australia. I didn't want to leave Steve. He was doing all he could to make me happy, and when I was straight I loved him.

It finally dawned on me that I was now an adult – technically, at any rate – and now there was a way I could stay in Australia. Simple. All I had to do was marry an Australian. Why not? Steve was happy to do it. We got stoned in the morning and married in the afternoon, and spent the wedding night completely out of our heads. Not quite the romantic start to a marriage my mother would have wanted for me. Not what I would have wanted for myself if I'd been half-way straight, but drugs take over. Nothing matters.

Marriage allowed me to stay in Australia. I had what I wanted, and so it wasn't long before I wanted something else. Life still wasn't the way it should be. There was a hole in it, and in my sane moments I was missing my parents. I needed a geographical. A trip to London would solve everything. I took some acid before going to the airport, and for most of the flight I was higher than the plane.

The day I got home, I must have looked like the letters I'd been sending – clean and healthy, fit and suntanned. The drugs didn't show. Another user might have known, but all my parents saw was a brown face and a big grin, and all they heard was a censored version of my brilliant career in Australia, the young housewife making a home. The lies came easily; by then I'd had plenty of practice, and I could put on a happy front when I got dressed for the day.

I'd heard through the users' grapevine where my old boyfriend and speed supplier was living, and I decided to go round and have a snort for old times' sake. From then on, every morning I'd kiss my mother goodbye and go out to score.

In parts of London at that time there were entire streets of squats – empty, derelict houses that had two great attractions: you could break into them with a screwdriver, and you didn't pay rent. The drug community took them over and the dealers moved in, turning the squat streets into addicts' shopping centres. That's where I went shopping. We used to call it the home for wayward boys and girls.

My old boyfriend was in a squat with his new girlfriend, and I had a welcome-home snort. The atmosphere was friendly, relaxed, no pressure. Straight people imagine junkie hotels to be permanently dangerous, edgy places, but they're not. As long as everyone is paying and everyone is scoring there's no more excitement than you'd find in a public library. It's only when someone tries to stiff a supplier or dealer that the men come round with sawn-off shotguns and sharpened bicycle chains and bottles of acid and start kicking doors down. Or there's the occasional panic when

19

a user overdoses. But normally, squat life is calm, even quiet. Addicts love company, they love getting stoned with other addicts. They're too busy hustling and getting high to look for trouble.

I never thought of myself as an addict then. I was just a heavy user looking for something. I didn't know what it was, but I knew that once I'd found it I could control my moods and feelings, my whole life. No depressions, no confusion, no black days, no problems, I'd be free of them all. And I'd be in charge. I never accepted that drugs were already controlling me. All I was doing was going through the menu, trying everything. One day I'd hit magic, and then I could start living the happy life. It's amazing how you can kid yourself.

I used to go down to the squat nearly every day, telling my parents I was setting something up. I always had a story, some innocent reason to explain why I was out all the time. Either I was trying to start a stall in the market, or I was making contacts in the music business for Steve, or I was going to import boomerangs and export Christmas puddings, always something. I seemed healthy and happy enough. The front was still up. To my mother and father, it must have looked as though I was really working at getting work.

The people in the squat fascinated me. They were older, more interesting and more exciting than the other friends I used to have. There were new people coming through the door all the time, and I had the feeling that any day now something would happen to change my life. And I was right.

I met David. He was tall, blond, wonderful blue eyes, dressed in black leather, a real street hero. Maybe I didn't quite throw myself at him, but I didn't run in the opposite direction, and suddenly that was it: Mrs Housewife from Australia started having her first affair. I don't remember even the slightest feelings of guilt. Drugs had numbed them as well as self-discipline and honesty, and I was able to explain it to myself with another convenient piece of addict's logic. I loved Steve and I loved David. Steve wasn't here and David was. I needed David, and what I needed I had to have, whether it was a quick hit or a warm body in bed. Why fight it? Not that I ever considered fighting it. I'd kicked that habit a long time ago.

Squat life went on, stoned, friendly squat life. Nobody seemed to be doing anything except grass or hash or speed or LSD, but I began to notice that from time to time, usually in the evenings, the house would go quiet. Rooms would be empty. It always happened when a man called the Doctor came round. Later on, the house would be full again and there would be a different feeling in the air. Everyone would be very well, very loose, very calm. Everyone except me.

I asked David what was going on, but he wouldn't tell me. I asked him again and again. What were they all doing? Who was the Doctor?

Why did he come to the house? Tell me or I'll leave you. Tell me. In the end, he did.

Smack.

The word, just the word, sounded like a big hit. Smack was the Doctor's prescription, and the patients were responding very well to treatment. His heroin clinic was a sell-out every time.

There it was, the secret of life, right under my nose. This was the drug for me. It must be. I'd tried all the others, and none of them did it, not for long enough. There was still a hole in my life. Grass and hash and speed and cocaine and downers and mushrooms and LSD and booze hadn't filled it, but heroin might. Let me try some. I've got to try some.

David did all he could to stop me. Smack was heavy, it was dangerous, it got you into using needles and sometimes it got you into the cemetery. The more he told me, the more I wanted to do it. I begged him and I bullied him and I threatened him and I won.

It seems almost funny to me now, but at that time I didn't have the guts to put the needle in by myself, so David had to do it for me. He borrowed some works from a friend and I rolled up my sleeve. I waited for half an hour while he dug around trying to get into the vein. The needle was old and blunt, and it hurt. I was in a kind of spasm of pain and impatience and excitement. Find the vein, for God's sake. Let me see that first drop of blood in the syringe.

He hit the vein, and within seconds the smack

hit me. It came from my belly like cream and spread everywhere – warm, calm, dreamy, filling me up with a sensation that was like nothing I'd ever felt before. The relief was overpowering, as if I'd finally come home after a long time away. It was love at first fix and the start of a long nightmare.

3

HOOKED

I woke up and felt like a hospital case, either too much of something the night before or not enough, I wasn't sure. Bad head, bad aches, bad all over. Shit.

Then room service arrived. The Doctor kicked the door open and stood in the doorway grinning, his eyes rolling, a fixing belt tied round his head and a loaded syringe in each hand.

'Come and get it! Start the day with a bang!'

I held out my arm and he told me what nice poppy veins I had, just like a man's. He took the belt from his head and tightened it round my arm, and hit the vein first time. He was good like that. Smack for breakfast, the beginning of another day in the squat.

I was using heroin whenever I could get hold of it, and whenever I could find someone to stick in the needle. It could be clean or dirty or blunt.

I didn't care about that, but I still couldn't shoot up on my own.

In between fixes, I was missing Steve, missing Australia. London was cold and grey, the perfect climate for depression. After three months of it, I needed travel, and this time I thought I'd found a way to make it pay. In London, hash was cheap and easy to get. In Australia, it was scarce and expensive. All I had to do was to smuggle it in. I worked out the details with David.

We found a small plaster statue in a junk shop, packed the hollow inside with hash and sealed up the bottom. It was the kind of obvious hiding place that you find on page one of the book on How To Be A Customs Officer, but we thought it was brilliant. And to make sure I didn't get caught, I decided not to take the statue with me; David would send it through the post. I wanted to take a little product to use as a sales sample, so I made a tampon the size of a cigar out of hash wrapped in sellotape, and hid it in my vagina. That's probably on page one of the book as well, but I had beginner's luck.

Steve met me in Melbourne, and I remember the shock on his face when he saw me. I'd left Australia tanned and healthy and come back a wreck – sick, thin and raving about drugs, this great stuff I'd been doing in London, these great people I'd met, this great scam I had going which would make us rich. He was shattered, but I hardly noticed. I was out of my head. I didn't know it then, but I was doing my first cold turkey.

My body wasn't getting its smack ration, and it was letting me know it wanted some more.

All the books say that cold turkey is no worse than a bad dose of flu, but I've never had flu like that. My bones felt soft and bruised, my muscles were sore as if they'd been hammered, my skin felt like an exposed nerve. Everything looked sharp and hard and painful. Everywhere hurt with a deep, deep ache. When I closed my eyes they stayed open, looking into the back of my head. I couldn't sleep. I threw up. I was in a constant cold sweat. My legs twitched, my eyes poured tears, my nose ran. My brain was screaming for a hit. It lasted about ten days, and then I turned bright yellow.

Nobody bleached their needles in the squat, and I must have taken a fix from dirty works. There had been so many needles in the past three months; one of them had given me hepatitis and the junkie's tan that goes with it. I stayed in bed for a month, my mind and body aching for smack. There wasn't any, so I made Steve get me acid, the best acid, and I spent two weeks drifting in and out of a trip, thinking it would clear out my system. And somehow, God knows how, I recovered.

The parcel of hash finally arrived, and made it through Customs. The word went round Melbourne like a snake on speed, and I sold out. I sat on the bed with the biggest pile of cash I'd ever seen. We'd done it, and it had been no more difficult than sending a Christmas present to your auntie. I called David and asked him to get another statue, more hash and don't forget to lick the stamps. We were in business.

Steve didn't like it at all. Why did I need to do this? Why take the risk? Why not get a job and stick to smoking grass and taking weekend trips on LSD, the way we used to? Why had I changed?

I didn't know. All I knew was that my life, my important, unique life, wasn't right. The money from smuggling hash would give me a chance to forget about earning a living, give me the time to think – about myself, my problems, my unhappiness, my future, me, me, me. My body may have taken a beating from hepatitis and heroin, but my ego was healtier than ever.

Everything was set for the second delivery of hash. My customers were ready with the dollars and I knew I could unload the whole lot in twenty-four hours. I worked out how much I was going to make and mentally put it under the mattress. Maybe the third shipment should be bigger – a family of statues, Mr and Mrs Hash and their fifteen children. This was money for nothing.

There was a knock on the front door one morning, and a man on the doorstep holding a parcel. A nice man. He smiled.

'Is this yours?'

I looked at the name and address. David's writing. This was it, a bundle of money wrapped up in brown paper. I told the man yes and reached for the parcel, and then from nowhere half a dozen plainclothes police were suddenly at the door, kicking it open, knocking me out of the way, going through the house like a pack of dogs. It was a bust. The hash queen of Melbourne was hauled off to the station and charged.

A date was set for the hearing, and I found a lawyer. He was very sympathetic, very reassuring. This was a first offence, I was young and he was confident he could straighten it all out. No worries, he said, but it's going to cost you. I gave him all the money I'd made from the first hash deal and never saw him again. His office said he'd gone bankrupt.

Now what? Finding another lawyer wouldn't be difficult, but finding the money to pay him was going to be something else. Lawyers are never cheap, the hearing was only a few weeks away and I was cleaned out. Steve was hardly making enough to keep us in grass. I needed a lot in a hurry, and I wasn't going to get it by working as a waitress.

*   *   *

The ad in the back of the Melbourne paper said 'JUST MODELS', and there was a telephone number, nothing else. I called to make an appointment, and went round to a neat suburban house in a quiet street. It was a house like hundreds of others in Melbourne except for the Alsatian chained up in the front yard. He was big and he looked underfed and mean, all teeth and growls.

The man who owned the house sat me down

and told me about his employment scheme for young ladies. He was a professional photographer and this was his sideline. He'd turned the house into a series of room sets – black rooms, mirrored rooms, leopardskin rooms, all with professional lighting equipment. It had cost him heaps, he said, but luckily there were hundreds of keen amateur photographers in Melbourne who liked to rent the rooms and take pictures. Nothing heavy, just blokes having a bit of fun.

I wasn't quite sure what he meant by a bit of fun, so he spelt it out for me. Nobody wants to take pictures of empty rooms, so he provided girls as part of the service. Art poses, he said. All perfectly respectable. If any of the punters got a bit frisky he brought in the Alsatian. There was nothing to worry about, he paid good money and his girls didn't even have to dress up to come to work. In fact, clothes weren't necessary.

I was desperate enough to have started there and then, but it was a slow day. I agreed to come back for the weekend trade.

When I told Steve, he looked as though I'd kicked him, hurt and angry. He couldn't believe I was prepared to roll around naked in front of any man who came through the door, but I'd made up my mind. I had to have the money. I probably kicked him again when I said I wouldn't do it if he could find enough to pay the lawyer. I knew he couldn't, and he knew he couldn't, and that made it worse. I must have been a gas to live with. It still amazes me that he never threw me out.

My first day at work was spent wrestling with one of the other girls while the punter took his pictures. I kept trying to cover my face until my wrestling partner told me to forget it. They're not interested in your face, she said. Stick your ass in the air and think of the money. I was grateful to her, because over the weeks she taught me to treat it like a game, to separate what I was doing from what I was thinking.

I'd lie there on the black bed hearing the *click, click, click* of a stranger's camera, and I'd be miles away. I was doing grass and speed and coke, but more and more I was thinking, dreaming about smack – that great ooze of warmth from the belly and the instant happiness. Let me just get over the court case and I'd sort myself out. *Click*. Turn over. *Click*. Put your leg this way. *Click*. Stretch out. *Click*. Kneel up. OK, OK. Why not?

I got the money and an honest lawyer, and my case came up. For drug offences that involved less than a certain amount – I think it was about £2000 – you were tried by a magistrate. Anything over that and you got a jury. Juries were known to be hard on drug offenders, and the police had exaggerated the value of the bust to make sure I had a jury trial. They were sure I was part of a ring, and they wanted me put away.

But something must have gone wrong, because I came up in front of a magistrate. I was stoned, but to him it could have looked as though I was just nervous. He said it was obvious that I wasn't part of an international drug ring, merely a misguided young girl. A sentence in the Melbourne Women's Prison might do more harm than good. Two years' Conditional, and don't let it happen again.

Conditional meant that if I kept out of trouble for two years I would be off the hook altogether, and the police were furious. They had tried to get a jury trial, and failed. Now they'd lost the case. They'd caught a dope smuggler red-handed and she was walking off with a slap on the wrist. They decided to appeal the verdict, and if the appeal was accepted they wanted a jury trial.

I had to get out of Australia before the appeal was heard. I'd been told about how tough it was in the Melbourne Women's Prison, and I was scared. I was also broke. All the money from art poses had gone to the lawyer, and I was scrabbling around for enough to score. A plane ticket to London was what I needed. London was safe. London had smack. And London was the home of the family bank. I called my mother.

She has a very direct sense of humour, my mother. I told her I was really missing her and my father badly – so badly I'd get on a plane tomorrow if they sent the money for a ticket. All I wanted was to come home, not soon, but now.

My mother laughed.

'What's the matter? Are the police after you?'

Yes, Mama, yes. Send the bloody money. Please. Of course, I didn't say that. It would have given the game away, so I told her that the air fare could be my birthday present. I was coming up to nineteen, and we could have a family celebration, a cosy birthday party. My mother said she'd send the money, and I hid in the house, not answering the door, until it arrived.

My last three birthdays had passed in a daze of dope, but I remember my nineteenth because I had it twice. I left Australia, high on STP (a kind of LSD), on 23 July. Steve said goodbye, worried and miserable. When I landed in London, it was 23 July again, and David met me at the airport. He'd bought a present of birthday coke. It was the first time I'd had it injected and the rush was smooth and deep. Many happy returns.

I got home a little late for the family celebration, but at least I got home, high on coke and relief at having ducked the Australian police. To my parents, it must have looked like normal excitement at seeing them again, and the tiredness from coming down could have been the natural effect of a long plane trip. Whatever people say, it's not easy or obvious to spot an addict unless you know what to look for.

My parents didn't. They knew I smoked grass, but most young prople in London smoked grass. I had wild mood swings brought on by drugs, but I was young, I didn't know what I wanted to do, I was still growing up – to a straight person, even someone close like a parent, the signs of addiction are often not that different from the emotional ups and downs that most teenagers go through on their way to becoming adults.

And I was careful with my lies and my disguise.

All my clothes had long sleeves to hide any fresh needle marks, all my days spent scoring were covered by stories of casual, untraceable jobs. It would have taken someone suspicious and familiar with addiction to find me out, and my parents were neither. They trusted me, and I conned them for years. Thousands of kids are conning their parents every day.

Steve followed me to London, and followed me into squat life. He hated me doing smack, and what smack was doing to me. We always had the same argument, and when he begged me to give it up I always gave him the same answer: you've never tried it, you don't understand what it's like. What I was really saying to him was join the club. Try it. You'll love it, like I do. Then you'll understand. Go on. Have a fix.

I can't imagine what I must have put him through, what blackmail I used on him to make him give in, but at last he agreed to try. We shot up together, the young married couple sharing everything, for better or for worse.

He liked smack. I knew he would. I couldn't believe that anyone wouldn't like it. But he didn't *love* it, the way I did, and I've since found out something I wish I'd known years ago.

I knew from the start that drugs affect different people in different ways. The highs aren't the same for everyone, and the physical reactions can vary enormously. The first hit of smack, for instance, can make some people retch and feel sick. That never happened to me, with smack or anything else. Whatever I used, I like instantly – grass, hash, speed, coke, LSD – they all worked in their own way to get me high. I don't think I ever had a bad first reaction to any drug. Worse than that, I had wonderful reactions to them all, physically and mentally. I used to think it was just me, lucky, special me. I now know that I was like millions of other addicts who have, maybe from birth, something called the X-factor.

Nobody knows exactly what it is or why some people have it and others don't, but what it does is no mystery. If you have the X-factor, your response to drugs will be supernormal. Instead of floating, you'll be in outer space. Instead of a rush, you'll have an explosion. Instead of being able to take drugs or leave them, you'll be hooked. The X-factor is in your body, waiting to be fed, as much a physical part of you as the colour of your eyes or the size of your nose, and if you don't know you've got it you're in trouble.

I didn't know that then, and I couldn't understand why Steve wasn't getting the same charge out of smack that I was. But he would, I knew he would, if he tried some more, and it wasn't long before I was scoring for two.

There was no bargain heroin in those days, and it was costing a small fortune. I was doing anything up to one and half grammes a day, and our smack bill was at least £500 a week, often much more. In 1980, that was a big lump to hustle or steal. I thought about modelling – art poses, *Vogue* covers, I wasn't fussy – and made appointments which I never kept. I didn't like to leave the squat without having a fix for the road, and once I'd had a fix I didn't want to leave.

Money was the problem of the day, the junkies' morning crisis. We all used to look down our noses at the rich kids who sometimes came to the squat to score, with their nervous laughter and their pockets full of Daddy's money. What did they know about real life? We had to go out and make it ourselves, and we were getting frantic.

One of the dealers had a French girlfriend, Eliane. She came from Marseille, which in the junkie world is not a bad background, rather like an expensive education. Eliane was never short of money, and she told me how she got it. She worked the clubs as a hostess, 'entertaining' tired businessmen who were away from home and looking for a little glamour. All she had to do was talk to them or dance with them. The clubs paid quite well, and the businessmen sometimes tipped. It sounded easy.

They're sad places, those clubs. If the men don't want to grope you, they want to tell you their life history, so you either have bruises or sore ears by closing time. The girls are told to keep smiling, to keep leaning forward so the punter has a nice view, to keep filling up the glasses with cheap champagne in high-priced bottles. The more drink you can push down them, the happier the club owner is, and the more popular you are.

My hours were from eight in the evening until

three or four in the morning, which is a long time to keep smiling even when you're stoned. I worked in seven or eight different clubs, one of them where the girls were topless. Funnily enough, it seemed to make the men shy. When you're wearing a low-cut dress, they can't stop trying to look down it, but when you're wearing nothing they look everywhere except at what's staring them in the face. I never understood that.

It was deeply boring work, and the money wasn't enough to pay for two habits. Thanks to me, Steve was addicted now, and he was more or less out of it as far as work was concerned. I needed better pay, faster money.

I'd noticed that some of the girls would sometimes go off with their punters when the club closed. Officially, this was forbidden because the club didn't want any problems with the police. The manager was always saying he ran a proper establishment, no monkey business. But when a girl and a punter went off together he looked the other way, or stuck his nose in the till to count the bar takings.

I talked to Eliane about it. She called it 'going case'. You went back to the hotel with the man, did the necessary and left with your handbag full of cash. One week she'd made nearly £1000.

£1000 a week would pay for my smack, and Steve's. That's all I could think about, or all I wanted to think about. No more anxiety sweats in the morning, no more shooting up with low-grade stuff cut with glucose, or worrying about whether it had been cut with something worse, like brick dust. We'd be able to afford the best, safest, cleanest heroin in town, piles of it.

Whenever any thoughts came into my head about what was involved in going case, I pushed them away. I remember telling myself it would be no worse than doing art poses in Melbourne. I had been mentally somewhere else then, and I could do the same now. I told myself I was making a choice, but of course I wasn't. I could no more make a choice than go through a day without a fix.

Steve went crazy. We fought and we screamed at each other with a blind, terrible addict's focus. The fights were mostly about different ways of getting money, hardly ever about giving up, getting out, going straight. Steve would say there must be some other way to get the money. I'd say, what other way? He didn't know. Then I told him what a junkie had once told me: when you're an addict, you either steal or you deal or you sell your ass. Fuck it. That's what I was going to do.

4

GOING DOWN

He was quite young. He looked normal and clean. He'd come over to London on business from Sweden, didn't know anyone, didn't know where to go for a good time. He'd walked past the club once or twice before he worked up the nerve to come in. A dream punter, harmless and shy, the kind who wouldn't complain when the bill arrived for the bad champagne. Maybe I could get two bottles down him before closing time.

He said he was lonely, which was something I used to hear a dozen times a night. When he'd had enough champagne to drown his shyness he asked me if I'd go back with him to his hotel. He said he had plenty of money.

I was so green I hadn't thought what I should charge. How many times would I have to do this to make £1000 a week? Were they all going to be the same as him, pleasant and straight? What was it going to be like? God, if only I could have a quick hit. Then it wouldn't matter what it was like.

On the way back to the hotel we didn't say much. I could feel he was nervous, and so was I. I hoped he wasn't going to change his mind. I needed the fix.

There was one moment, sitting on the edge of the bath in the hotel, 'getting ready', when I had second thoughts. This wasn't going to bed stoned for fun or love or a fast fling with someone I found attractive. Amateur nights were over. This was professional, screwing for money. I'll give you my body. You give me your wallet. I remember thinking that if I went through with it there would be no easy way to turn back. Once or a thousand times, what's the difference when you've stepped over the line? One stranger's the same as the next.

I'm here. I need the money. I need another fix. All I have to do is open the bathroom door and get on with it.

He hardly touched me before it was over, alcohol and nervousness and embarrassment. He said he was sorry. It was the first time he'd ever done anything like this. He gave me £120, and I went out and scored.

I'd done it, and I told myself it would always be that easy, that quick, that meaningless, five minutes of nothing. As I said, I was green.

*   *   *

My hash-dealer friends next door had a proposition. They had planned to get out of London for a few months and try getting high in Morocco; they asked me if I'd like to take over their squat and their contacts and keep everything warm for them while they were away. It was only hash, but at least it was steady, so Steve and I moved in and took over.

If you're dealing like we were at the bottom end of the market and using at the top end, it takes less than twenty-four hours to go broke. The profits from hash don't come anywhere near the outlay on smack. We decided we had to expand the dealership, to take on heroin and anything else we could get our hands on, and feed our habits free. It wasn't difficult. Wholesalers are always happy to take on new dealers, and we were only dealing in small amounts, the scum end of the market. We dropped the word in the squat grapevine one day, and the customers were there the next. References weren't necessary, and trust didn't come into it. Everyone knew that if you play games you'll end up getting cut or shot or with a face full of acid or two broken legs. Those are the rules. Usually, there's no trouble.

I was going case as often as I could to pay for our stock and I found out how lucky I'd been with the young Swedish businessman. I learned that I had to get the money first, while I still had my clothes on. I learned never to leave my clothes in the bathroom, because there were times when it was dangerous to hang around and I had to get out fast. I learned to keep condoms in my handbag as some kind of protection against the clap. I learned to shut the eyes of my mind to what I was doing. I learned to be a piece of meat.

That was work, and after that dealing was a pleasure. Give me a junkie any time over a businessman; you know where you are with junkies.

I used to sit in the squat weighing out the grammes on these scales, beautiful old scales, and making up the bags. I was very neat about it, very professional. One day I wanted to have a black leather attaché case with special compartments: one for hash, one for speed, one for coke, one for smack, and maybe a row of clean syringes with sharp, first-time needles. I could see myself going out on calls, Doctor Feelgood with her attaché case. It was part of kidding myself that I was leading a normal life.

In fact, life had become completely reversed. For me, normality was the squat, living among junkies whose only interests were money, hustling, scoring and fixing. That was safe and familiar. The ordinary world, filled with ordinary people, was strange and dangerous. The police were my enemies, the businessmen I met on night work were often freaks and my parents were slipping away. They tried to stay close to me and I pushed them off, knowing that if they got too close they'd find out. I told myself I didn't want to hurt them with the truth, so I hurt them with lies instead. Didn't they understand? I was too busy to see them.

Working the clubs was driving me crazy, taking up too much time. The men knew what they were there for. I knew what I was there for. Why did we have to go through all those hours of conversation before doing the business? Sometimes I'd try to hurry them along, but unless they'd had a skinful of champagne they'd get nervous and duck off, and I'd end up with nothing except a hangover and a handbag of unused condoms. I was sick of it, sick of smiling nicely, sick of leaning forward and feeling their eyes slither down me, sick of their stupid cocky grins and their dirty jokes.

Most of the other girls felt the same way. We talked about it a lot in between listening to the punters, and one girl said if I'd really had it with the clubs I should try the car trade – go out on the street, pick up the crawlers, park in an alley and do it. She said there wouldn't be much conversation.

Everyone told me that Soho was too rough for a beginner, so I picked Queensway. I could walk to Queensway from the squat, it was a wide, bright street, always plenty of traffic, a good, sleazy beat.

I've never been so frightened as I was that first night. I suddenly realised the risks I was taking, and getting arrested was the least of them. When a strange man has you in his car you're shut off from help. He might be a sad little creep or a psycho with a razor, but he's got you in a cage for as long as he keeps driving. And when he stops, somewhere dark, somewhere deserted, he may want sex or he may want to beat you up, or both. He can do anything. He knows you're not going to file a complaint with the police.

I walked down Queensway looking for crawlers, terrified. Don't get in the car if there are two men in it. Don't get in if the man looks weird, or like a plainclothes. How can you tell in the dark if a man looks weird? Don't walk too slowly or the police might pick you up. Don't walk too fast or the crawlers won't clock you. Make eye contact with the drivers. Don't look scared. Stop trembling.

There was a car coming towards me, five miles an hour. It pulled into the kerb and stopped. As I walked up to it, the passenger door opened and the driver leaned over. He was alone. He just looked at me. I got in, and he drove away from the lights, into a side road.

He didn't know London, he said. He was from Egypt, said he was a policeman, learning about English methods of crime prevention. Did I know somewhere quiet and dark where he could park? That's one of the advantages of working Queensway; there are plenty of dark places round the back.

It was disgusting but it was quick. He gave me £20 and asked me if I wanted to come to Cairo. He'd find me work. I got out of the car and threw up.

*   *   *

The hash dealers came back from Morocco and Steve and I had a housing problem. We had to move out, and all the other squats were full.

We didn't want much: a mattress on the floor, a table for the scales, a place to hide the gear and no rent. As I'd done so many times before, I went to my parents with a sob story. Steve was finding it hard to get work, I was doing the best I could with odd jobs, but we couldn't scrape up enough money for the rent. A few hundred pounds a week for smack wasn't part of the story. If only we could find somewhere for a few months we'd be able to get back on our feet.

I suppose they must have looked at me – thin, pale, desperate, begging – and felt sorry for me. We hadn't been getting on, but in the end I was their daughter, their only child, going through a bad time. They thought my marriage wasn't working out. That's why I was losing weight, that's why I'd been so distant. Poor, miserable Raffaella.

Some friends of theirs happened to be out of the country for six months, and their flat – right next door to my parents – was empty. We could move in there until the friends came back. My mother was delighted. She could see more of me, she could make sure I ate properly, we could get close again. She showed me round the flat, and I checked it for hiding places. The front door was at the back of my parents' house, so I could come and go without them knowing. So could my customers. Perfect. Even though I'd only be a few yards away from my mother and father, I could carry on dealing. We moved in.

I was a big girl now, and I was able to inject myself. As well as smack I started fixing cocaine, shooting it straight into the vein, getting the rush within seconds, but getting the comedown within minutes. It never lasted long enough. There were times when I'd have a fix before going out, hide the works, get to the door and then panic at the thought of the fix wearing off. Back to the needle for more. I was using two grammes a day, and I was paying for it the only way I could, working Queensway.

By now, I'd become hardened to it, or numb. Whatever happened in the cars, in the alleys, in the park, in the blackness under the bridges with the traffic passing overhead, I didn't care any more as long as it was quick. I gave up underwear, left it at home when I went out to work. The crawlers weren't interested in underwear, and I could work more quickly without it. Get in the car, get it over with, get the money, get out, look for the next one. Another £20, another fix.

I never let them kiss me. That was personal. From the neck down was business.

Out of all the men, I have good memories of one. He had a Porsche, which is a cramped, difficult car to work in. Then he started to talk, so I tried to get out. I didn't get paid for talking. He asked me what I made on a good night, and said he'd give it to me if I'd have dinner with him, so I did. It felt strange, sitting in the restaurant like a normal couple on a date. I'm sure I was the only girl there without any underwear. After dinner he drove me home, but I wouldn't let him kiss me.

I was getting very thin and very paranoid. My father spent hours talking to me, trying to find out what was wrong, his face bunched up with worry. I was careful to keep my sleeves rolled right down and tried not to scratch my nose too often.

The talks never got anywhere. They couldn't. I wouldn't tell him the truth, and he hadn't guessed it, so we used to sit there, two sad and worried people. He worried about me; I worried about the next fix. Addiction is a disease that infects the whole family, and it was infecting my father. In the end, his worry would turn to frustration and I'd go next door and shoot up.

The nights were bad. I knew someone was coming to get me, someone was there outside, waiting. I used to double lock the door and push a heavy chair against it. Then I could have a fix. But I couldn't go to sleep, because if I went to sleep they'd come for me. So I'd have another fix and get a kitchen knife and stand with my back to the wall, staring at the door until the night was over and they went away. They wouldn't come in the daytime. They only came in the dark.

I couldn't go on living next door to my parents. They'd find out. They were probably spying on me, trying to catch me fixing up. I didn't trust them. I didn't trust anyone except Steve. I had to get out, back to a squat, back to safety, away from people who said they loved me and worried about me. Fuck *them*.

Pack up the scales, pack up the gear, go through the stashes in the flat to make sure nothing was left, check behind the lavatory in case there were any syringes and needles taped to the back, say goodbye, move on, kick the parents in the teeth again and run away.

They thought it was Steve's fault. He was older, and I suppose they felt that his influence was behind everything I'd become and everything I did. They didn't know that he was a junkie, and that I'd helped to turn him into a junkie, or that I was making the decisions because I was making the money. Steve couldn't work Queensway.

So we left to go back to squat street without any fond farewells. One daughter, two parents, three strangers.

*　　*　　*

I was dealing like a maniac during the day and practically flagging down cars on the street at night to pay for our habits. I might as well have been mainlining £10 notes every five minutes, day in and day out. I'd started to use drugs for the pleasure they gave, but there wasn't much pleasure now. Now they were a relief from the pain of what I was doing to myself, a few minutes of escape from filthy surroundings and men in cars and no hope and no self-respect. I was treating the disease with more of the same disease. Obviously, it got worse.

I think I had my twenty-first birthday party in the back of a car with a man who stiffed me for the money afterwards, but that was my fault. I should have taken the money first. I was too tired to get angry for long, too numb to do anything except look for another car. I didn't really have feelings any more when I was awake.

But I used to dream, and one night I dreamed about the time I'd spent in Italy as a child, with my mother's family. It was sunny and noisy with laughter. I was allowed to drink a glass of red wine cut with water, and it made me feel giddy. Everyone thought it was funny, little Raffaella getting tipsy on a teaspoon of wine, and they ruffled my hair and hugged me and then we went down to the beach and I went to sleep on the hot sand. Someone carried me back to the house. I felt very safe.

It was like a nightmare in reverse when I woke up. Reality was the nightmare – the dirty mattress, the dirty squat, the dirty needles, getting out on the street hoping I wasn't too thin for the crawlers, the feeling that if I didn't get a fix I'd go mad. Shit. I've got to give this stuff up. I'm a slave.

I had a hit to help me think about it.

I'd get away from London, stay with my relatives in Italy, get clean, eat properly, be normal. Almost normal, anyway. I couldn't face doing cold turkey again, so I'd use methadone and pills to help me come off gently. Six weeks of methadone and I wouldn't need heroin any more. Six weeks, and then I could start putting my life together.

I lasted fourteen days in Italy, and it felt like a year. I couldn't wait to get back to London and score. It was pathetic. I hated myself, and the only way I could stop hating myself was to get high.

I lived on smack and cigarettes. Food was the last item on the shopping list, and only if there was some money left over. If there wasn't, I stole from supermarkets. I started wearing baggy sweaters so that nobody would see how thin I was. I didn't want to look at my body, so I stopped taking baths. I stank. I was getting more paranoid, and carried a knife in case they came to get me.

I seesawed between heroin, methadone, coke and any junk I could find, but it was no good. A day, two days and I was shaking for a hit of smack.

Some of the dealers liked playing games with me. They'd fix a time and make me wait, not answering the door, not hearing me scream through the letterbox, just so I understood that they had the power to keep me on the end of the string as long as they felt like it. I always waited. I had to. One night I spent six hours in the rain, standing on the pavement, unable to take my eyes off the window of the dealer's room. I knew he was up there. He knew I was down on the street. Fucking bastard.

I would have waited all night, but the police came and picked me up for loitering. One of them looked at me and shook his head. You're a junkie, he said, a useless, bloody junkie. What are you on? I told him methadone and he said he wanted the bottle, if I didn't take him home and get it he'd break the door down. I took him back and gave him the methadone.

He asked me how old I was, and when I told him 'twenty-one', he said I hadn't got long to go, I'd never make it to twenty-five. I believed him. I knew I couldn't go on much longer, but I didn't know what to do, or the will to do it. I just accepted that I was going to die young. So what? Living meant nothing. I wouldn't miss much.

I was resigned to it, so I became careless. I used anything, in any amount, the more of it the better. If Steve hadn't rationed me, if he hadn't hidden junk where I couldn't find it, I would have killed myself before I was twenty-two. God knows I tried.

5

THE BOTTOM OF THE CURVE

The dealer we used to call the Poison Dwarf was lying on the floor, very still. I watched him as if I were watching television, remote and half-interested. I could see the skin on his face changing to a pale, greeny-yellow, the colour of dirty wax. This time he'd overdosed. He was always greedy.

I knew what to do – all junkies know what to do – but I hesitated to do it. I knew he was carrying twenty-five grammes on him. If I let him die I could take it, step over him and shut the door. I wouldn't have to go and score for days. Nobody would care. What's another dead junkie?, Sooner or later they'd find the body and take it away, and then I could come back to my room again.

I don't know why I didn't go through his pockets and run. I like to think it was my conscience twitching, but it was more likely that I didn't want the problem of finding somewhere else to sleep. I knelt over his body and saw the greasy shine of sweat on his face and gave him the emergency treatment: lift up the rib cage, thump on the chest, get the heart started again. I told myself that if it didn't work at least I'd tried. Then I'd be entitled to take whatever he had on him.

But he came round, fuck it. He wasn't even grateful, just worried that I'd taken some of his stuff while he'd been practising dying.

*   *   *

Addiction is a progressive disease, and it's sometimes shown in the books as the downward half of a curve, starting with occasional use for pleasure and ending with obsession and paranoia. My travels down the curve had taken nine years, and I hadn't missed a single step. I'd gone from soft drugs to hard drugs, from snorting and smoking to mainlining. I'd stolen and lied, and hurt everybody close to me. I'd tried to run away from myself by changing my surroundings, moving from country to country, from squat to squat, from dealing to prostitution. I'd used my body like a tip for chemical waste, and put my emotions to sleep. I'd been very thorough, a case history of slow suicide.

The books also show an upward half to the curve, the half that leads towards recovery and staying clean. I didn't know about that, but I wouldn't have believed it anyway. It wouldn't work for me. My problem was unique and incurable. It was going to be like the policeman said, all over by the time I was twenty-five.

Meanwhile, life of a sort went on, and I accepted it as the only life it was possible for me to lead. I remember watching a friend fixing up in the squat, mainlaining smack into the vein of his penis because his other veins had collapsed. It didn't seem anything special. Most of my friends had collapsed veins, and they had to learn to take their hits wherever they could.

I went to a junkies' party one night when someone had scored enough to celebrate. They're not very lively, junkies' parties, but it's nice to have the company. We sat around, smacked out of our heads, having a wonderful time. One of the girls was still out of it when we left, sitting on the floor with her back against the wall. The next morning someone shook her, and she just slid sideways. We hadn't noticed her dying, and didn't know how long she'd been dead, but if she had any gear or money left she wouldn't be needing it now. Someone called an ambulance.

Every minute spent outside the squat was torture, too much noise, too many people going too fast, too many enemies out to get me. Whenever I had to go and score I walked along sideways, my back against the wall like a rat. The only safe, good places were public toilets where I could fix up before going home. If they didn't have a basin that worked, I used to get water from the cistern,

53

and if I couldn't get the top off the cistern I used water from the toilet bowl.

I was still working Queensway. Crawlers aren't too choosy. Most days I stank. My hair was falling out. I'd stopped having periods, and I'd lost so much weight that my bones felt stripped and raw. My two hands met round the top of my thigh, and when I lay flat on the bed I could see my ovaries. Anything harder than a soft cushion gave me bruises. A rough crawler would have snapped me into little pieces.

I collected cigarette ends from the gutter to smoke the last shreds of tobacco. I used filters for fixing, to keep out any impurities, the careful junkie's recipe for cleaner hits. If anyone stopped to look at me, I'd beg for money, say I was sick, couldn't afford a doctor, couldn't afford a packet of cigarettes.

Everything was out of control, exactly the opposite of what I had hoped drugs would do for me. I'd hoped for freedom and put myself into a prison. I'd hoped for happiness and found misery. I'd hoped for an expanded world and more intense feelings and found narrowness, numbness, dulness and fear. I was frightened of emotions, frightened of straight people, frightened of life. I was living for the needle, and the small, short relief it brought.

My marriage was over, my husband was a junkie and my parents were two figures in the far distance, blurred, worried figures. We kept in touch from time to time by phone. I didn't want them to see me and I didn't want to see them. They'd make me feel guilty, and that I couldn't face.

They tried to get me to come home one Christmas, but I told them I was too busy. There were so many parties to go to that I couldn't fit them all in. That was the story. The truth was that I hated Christmas because all the dealers disappeared, so I scored as much as I could and went back to the squat on Christmas Eve, had a massive fix and went to bed. I smoked for a while and fell asleep. I woke in the middle of the night and watched the pretty colours flickering around the bed, red and orange among the shadows, soothing and dreamy. If a friend hadn't smelled the smoke and come up I would have been burnt to death. I still wonder if I would have felt anything. I don't know. I was numb from the neck up. I was numb from the neck down too, as long as I was stoned.

Even then, when it must have been obvious to other people, I never thought of myself as being sick in the sense of having a disease. Not me. I was a special, hopeless case, a loser. I'd given up on everything except scoring. There was no point to anything else and no future beyond the next fix. I thought about taking too much on purpose, shooting my system so full that it would explode after one colossal, terminal rush. A snowball would be the way to go, a double dose of coke and smack, the hit to end all hits.

I couldn't even do that: tired of life, scared of

55

death, the old story. An accident might put me away, but a deliberate act of will never would. Acts of will were few and far between in my life. I was repeating the same mistake, day after day, and expecting different results.

A long time later, I copied down two phrases. The first is 'an inability to manage one's own affairs and perform one's social duties'. The second is 'without recognition of one's own illness'. Both of those applied to me. They're definitions of insanity.

I was talking to my mother on the phone, one of the calls I'd make when I'd just had a fix and could put on a good act. How are you? I'm fine, everything's fine. How's Papa? How's the cat?

We're going away together, my mother said, you and me. She didn't ask. She told me. Someone had offered to lend her a house outside New York, on the beach at Fire Island, and I had a feeling she was going to take me there if she had to put me in a suitcase to do it.

I had a bath and put on my least dirty clothes and got stoned to help me through the flight. I had some pills, but I couldn't afford anything else, and I thought what a pity I was too broke to take some smack with me. Aircraft toilets are perfect for fixing up, clean and private, always plenty of water.

The place on Fire Island was beautiful, one of those simple wooden houses with big windows where the light pours in and a deck where you can sit out and listen to the sea. There was a pool,

56

it was very hot and I was covered up from the neck to the ankles. I'd always loved the sun and the water when I was a child – that was one of the reasons my mother had taken the house. She thought it would be good for me to swim and get some clean air and put on some weight, and she couldn't understand why I was staying in the shade wrapped up, with my nose in a book. She didn't know that my baggy clothes had to stay on, that the sun would hurt, that what was left of my body was starting to sweat and shiver and beg for heroin.

Why don't you come down by the pool? Why don't you get some colour? You're so pale.

My body aches. My eyes are sore. The sun's too bright. I need a fix.

No, I'm OK. I think I'll go inside and read.

The book made no sense. I was looking at the words, but they were just lines, jumpy, confusing lines of little black ants going back and forth across the page.

Need a fix. Need a fix. Need a fix.

I went to the bathroom to see if there was anything in the medicine cabinet above the basin. Bloody Band-Aid and Alka-Seltzer. I felt like smashing the mirror. I went back to the book, and the little black ants. Need a fix.

I couldn't have a fix.

I *had* to have a fix.

I couldn't stand it. I put the book down and went out to where my mother was reading by the pool. I stood there and took off my clothes, layer by layer, until I was naked. Just bones and needle marks. I started to cry.

'Mama, look at me.' I held out my arms, two bruised, perforated sticks. 'I'm a junkie, mama. I can't stop taking drugs.'

6

COMING OFF

I don't know what I was expecting: hysterics, anger, disgust, none of them would have surprised me. I deserved them. I'd done exactly what I wanted to do, it had gone bad and now I was feeling sorry for myself. I'd run out of lies and excuses and money and self-respect. I was a bag of bones standing in the sun giving my problems to somebody else.

My mother was amazingly calm. I know she was shocked, but I think she might have felt some relief that she finally knew why I was such a disturbed mess. A junkie in the family was somehow less hopeless than a lunatic. At least you can fight addiction, at least drugs are more tangible than insanity, although there's not much difference between the two.

My mother would have been good in a war. When there's a crisis, she doesn't waste time being dramatic; she gets very practical. She said that we'd go through cold turkey together, as though it were something she'd been doing all her life. I told her I needed some help from pills, and she somehow persuaded a doctor to give her enough to keep half of Fire Island stoned. Now I had Mama scoring for me.

The pills helped a little, enough for her to try to carry on some kind of normal life. She thought it would be a distraction for me to see other people, so she had friends round for dinner. I spent the evening in the bathroom in a cold sweat, throwing up.

I was losing more weight, almost too weak to walk. My mother called the narcotics Help Line in New York, and the voice told her I should get to a doctor, that there was the risk of a heart attack. An hour later we were on our way to the airport to go back to London. All I could think about on the plane was getting a fix, just one, just to help me get through the thing I was dreading most: I was going to have to tell my father. Mama wouldn't do it for me.

I said I had to pick up some clothes from the squat, and shot myself full of smack, one last hit to give me the guts to be honest.

It was as if I'd murdered part of the family, which I suppose I had. My father had no idea, he was nowhere near it, and even through the haze of smack I could see the pain on his face. The three of us sat round the kitchen table trying to work out the solution to a problem none of us knew anything about. All I knew was how to get hooked; coming off hadn't been part of my drug education.

We started where most people would have started, by going to see a doctor, and we talked about coming off with methadone. I knew two things about methadone: the withdrawal, when it's time to stop, is worse than cold turkey. And if you can get a doctor to give you methadone, you can always sell it to buy smack. That combination, for someone like me with the willpower of jelly, didn't sound like the answer.

The doctor made another suggestion. There were people who specialised in helping addicts recover, and he recommended two. I thought, as usual, that what worked for the rest of the world couldn't possibly work for someone as unique as me, but I said I'd go along and see one of them, Joyce Ditzler. She had trained at Guy's Hospital in London and worked at the Roosevelt Hospital in New York, and she and her husband had been treating addicts and alcoholics in Britain since 1975. I thought she sounded like some sort of crank. Who else would waste time with incurables like me?

I was stoned when I saw her the first time, and she knew it. I liked her. She didn't pat my hand and tell me what a poor unlucky girl I was. She was very direct and tough, and told me some good news and some bad news.

The bad news was for my ego. I wasn't unique. I wasn't a special case. She'd seen hundreds like me, all with similar inflated ideas of their own problems. Nobody had ever told me that before.

The good news was that I wasn't a terminal fuck-up with two or three years left to live. I was sick. I had a disease which could be treated, and there were thousands of cases where the treatment had worked. There was a way to get off drugs. There was a way to lead a normal, happy life.

Before I heard that, I had always divided people into three groups: straights, users and dead users. Now she was telling me there was a fourth group, recovered addicts, and if I didn't believe her I could go to a meeting of Narcotics Anonymous and see for myself. If I went to a treatment centre, if I went to NA, if I really wanted to get clean and stay clean, I could do it. Other addicts had done it. The success rate was 50% or more. She wasn't giving me theories. She was telling me facts.

I listened. I wanted to believe it and I wanted to come off drugs, but I didn't accept that I couldn't do it on my own. Stupid and stubborn. I thought I'd come off, but I'd come off by myself, in my own way. The ego wasn't giving up without a fight. I still felt that what had worked for other addicts wouldn't work for me. I'd spent years thinking that I was different and special; it was another habit which was going to die hard, unless I died first.

When in doubt, run away. I went on a camping holiday in France – a little tent, a little gas stove to cook on, a little methadone to keep me company. I'd be careful with it. I'd come down gradually. I'd stay away for two weeks and then I'd come back to London and get really clean, all by myself.

The first night was fine, but I used half the methadone I'd bought to last for two weeks. The second night I used the other half. The third night I was on a train back to London, thinking all through the journey of the quickest way to score some smack. By now I didn't kid myself I was scoring for pleasure; now it was for relief. Physically I was in pain and mentally I was a disaster. I'd stopped hoping that drugs would make me happy, but what else was there? I'd been stoned since I was twelve years old, so there was nothing from the past to make me think that life had any more to offer than being high.

Somewhere between France and London, coming and going through the craving for a fix, I had an attack of honesty. I'd tried cold turkey, I'd tried switching drugs, I'd tried changing boyfriends, I'd tried running away. Nothing had worked. Heroin was stronger than anything. Heroin was stronger than me. Once I'd finally admitted that, I had to admit that I couldn't stop using unless I had help. On my own against heroin, I'd lose. With other people to hold me up, maybe there was a chance. It was the first glimmer of sense I'd had for years.

I decided to try Narcotics Anonymous, and went to a meeting expecting to find a bunch of freaks. The room was fogged with cigarette smoke, and I sat the edge of the group and looked at my fellow addicts: businessmen, bricklayers, secretaries, housewives, people on the dole – they were a mixture from every kind of social background. And they weren't freaks. They were like me, except that most of them weren't using and I was. They were happy and I wasn't. I was on the wrong side of the window.

You don't give your last name at NA meetings, but if you want to come clean about everything else, and bring all the shit out into the open, you can. Some of the others were doing it, admitting that drugs were more powerful than they were, accepting that they had a disease.

I wasn't quite ready for that. I couldn't strip off and expose my life to a roomful of strangers. There had been too many years of hiding the truth, mostly from myself. I kept quiet, waiting for the meeting to be over so I could get away and have a hit.

But something stayed with me. For the first time, I had met addicts who had recovered. They hadn't died, they'd stopped using and they were living normal lives. They were still addicts and they would always be addicts, but they'd learned how to keep the disease from destroying them. If they could do it, other addicts could do it. Maybe even I could do it. It was strange, almost comfortable, to feel something I couldn't remember feeling before. Hope was a new experience.

My parents agreed that I should go into treatment. It cost about the same per day as a heavy smack habit, and they had to borrow the money to pay for it. I was twenty-three, and they were investing in the prospect of my reaching twenty-four.

I went into treatment as though I was going to the moon, with no idea of what it would be like. I couldn't imagine that straight people would spend their time helping addicts like me. But the counsellors were recovered alcoholics. They knew about addiction, and they were good – sympathetic but tough, rather like Joyce Ditzler had been. As usual, I did my best not to accept that I could be treated like everyone else. Twice I ran away, and twice they took me back. It was a confused, unreal time. My mind felt like water swirling around a sink, going nowhere, thinking nothing, numb. I was off drugs and I'd put on weight, but my brain was in a bandage.

The normal course of treatment used to last about six weeks. I was there, counting my two excursions, from 22 September to 31 December. Three months of being more or less clean. Progress.

I went back to London. Steve had left to go home to Australia. They said he'd stopped using. I should have felt happy for him, but it was as though one of my arms had been cut off. He'd been there since I was sixteen and I think he might have saved my life more than once. When I'd been too stoned to worry about an overdose, he'd been the brake. He'd loved me. In return, I'd given him a smack habit and years of unhappiness.

Now he was gone, and now drugs were gone, the other arm cut off. I felt like an eggshell with no egg inside. They'd taken away the drugs without putting anything back. Was this how it was going to be? Was this normal life?

I had to talk to someone who had been through it, but, stubborn and stupid, I didn't want to get help from NA. My way was better than their way. The truth was I still wanted to use, but I wasn't prepared to admit it. So I called a girl I'd met in treatment. She'd been in twice. She'd understand. She'd know what to do.

I went to see her, and we sat there telling each other how great it was to be straight, how it was all going to get easier, life was going to be OK. If we'd had long enough, we might have been able to convince each other. If one of her friends hadn't come round we might have stayed on coffee and cigarettes.

The friend was carrying a shopping bag. He'd just broken into a chemist's, and he had enough gear to open a supermarket. He spread it out on the table – pills, powders, shiny new needles – and we were off. Three months wiped out in five minutes.

*   *   *

Back on the seesaw. There might be a week or ten days of being clean and then I'd start using again, and start hating myself again. When I was straight I could see what I had to do, and it was simple: don't use today. Don't make promises about not using for three weeks or six months. Just don't use today. Go to bed clean. Wake up clean. Deal with life twenty-four hours at a time. Surely I wasn't too weak to do that.

The thought of going back on to heroin terrified me, and yet the thought of living without it terrified me. I knew it was possible because I'd seen addicts at NA meetings who had done it. Plenty of them. But they were winners, not losers like me. Every time I went to NA I came away with mixed feelings of envy and desperation, and desperation usually won. So I'd go and have a fix to make it better.

I was still seeing Joyce. She told me the least I could do was to be clean when I came to see her. I never was, I always lied about it, and she always knew. I wasn't kidding anyone except myself. She told me I had to get rid of my pride, get rid of my ego, get honest and get to NA. I knew it was good advice, and I resisted it as much as I could.

One morning I couldn't even kid myself any more. I woke up in a sweat, shaking. My mother came in with a cup of tea when all I wanted was an early morning needle, and I couldn't stop crying, couldn't stop shaking. My mother sat on the end of the bed and I had to tell her that I couldn't get up if I didn't have a hit.

She left the room while I fixed up, and when I came out she told me I was going to go back into treatment. They'd borrow more money and we'd try again.

I went back into treatment, this time to a centre about 120 miles from London, where it would be more difficult to slip round the corner and score.

As part of the treatment, we all had to tell our life stories, our histories of addiction, what we'd done to ourselves and to other people. It was different from NA: at NA, I could run out for a fix at the end of the meeting, and I could keep on ducking. In treatment, the pressure was on to tell the truth, all of it. Until you admit what you are and accept what you are – an addict, totally unable to control drugs – there is no hope of recovery. They used to say that the denial of powerlessness is the addict's insanity, and as long as you believe you have any control at all over drugs you'll never come off. The ego has to give in.

So we all told our stories. That was bad enough, but what was worse were the letters that came afterwards. Each of us had to write down what we thought about the other addicts and their lives. This is one letter I had, typical of them all:

'Dear Raffaella:
Thanks for letting me hear your life story, which has been like every other junkie story I've ever heard.

You rebelled at school, against your parents and against society, but everyone has a rebellious streak in them so I'm afraid you're not alone as a rebel. You stole from everyone around you to get your drug of choice, but all

68

junkies do things like that, so you're not alone as a thief. I wasn't even surprised that you turned to prostitution, as most female junkies do that to get a few bob for their little bag of smack.

Then you ran like a hare from one country to another, like most junkies do, because you couldn't face up to reality. Oh yes, you did some nude photography as well, wanking material for dirty old men. Would your parents be proud of you for doing this, or don't they know?

You even got married, that was nice, your mother and father must have been proud of you on your wedding day. Oh, I forgot. You rang them up and told them. They must have been very pleased. Also your wedding night must have been nice, you lying in bed out of your head and Steve lying there wanting to make love but he couldn't because of the state you were in. Or maybe the two of you were out of your heads because you seemed to introduce Steve to drugs.

You mentioned your sex life deteriorated. I don't think you ever had much of a sex life because you were out of your head most of the time. You caused a car accident, and said that you were hurt, but you never mentioned anyone else being hurt. Are human beings just objects to you? All your life you have been selfish and self-centred and taken care of yourself.

Also I don't buy that you are as quiet as you seem. I bet you're as hard as nails. You lived and slept around in squats and carried on using. But of course your Mum and Dad seem to have bailed you out of all the troubles you've got yourself into in life. They've given you everything and you've treated them like dirt. Do they deserve all the shit you've given them? But I forgot. They're just objects to you.

You've used your parents like a cashline card to get money for your drug of choice. They must really love and care for you to keep sending you to treatment centres, but eventually they'll disown you as they must be sick and tired of being used as a cash card. When I saw your parents I thought your Dad looked shattered. You are the only one your parents have got in their lives. If you overdosed and died from a bag of smack I don't think they could handle it.

Take this programme seriously and ask for advice and try not to do it on your own as you've done before. Honesty and trust have got me clean and sober. I sincerely hope you stay clean and sober this time.'

*   *   *

The weeks went by, and I did stay clean and sober. After three months, I was told I could have my own NA meeting, rather like graduating. During the treatment they had told me I should go for a year without having sex. For the first year of being clean, emotions are over-sensitive without drugs to deaden them, and being dumped by a man would be likely to send me straight back to using. But that didn't sound impossible. If I could do without drugs, I could do without sex. A day at time, and the year would pass.

I went off to the meeting and never got there. I bumped into Michael, who had been in treatment with me and gone back to using, and I caved in. Another three months of help and money disappeared down the drain in the time it took to fix up. I was hopeless. I couldn't face going back into treatment, getting more letters from addicts who were able to stay clean when I wasn't able to take a short bus ride without jumping on to a needle. I gave up, and moved in with Michael. And to spread the despair around, I called my mother and told her.

We talked for an hour and a half. I said I was going to register as an incurable addict and go on a methadone programme until I dropped. The next day I called again and said I'd changed my mind, and I was going to try again to come off; not now, but later. It must have been like the ramblings of a madwoman.

Within days, it was as if I'd never stopped using or lying. I worked my way through the local doctors with the same story: I've just moved down here, my husband's left me, I've had an abortion, I can't sleep, I can't get a job, I need

71

some pills. I always got them on the first visit. After that, the doctors realised I wasn't what I claimed.

When I ran out of doctors I started breaking into houses and taking the milk train up to London to sell the stuff and score. I was using anything I could get, any amount, any mixture. I overdosed twice. It didn't scare me enough to stop. Even knowing there was an alternative wasn't enough to make me stop. Numb from the neck up, just like the old days.

Six months of this, and I couldn't take any more of it, so I crawled back home to give my parents more grief. Again, they took me in. Again, they said we can beat it together. I don't know where they got the strength from. I'd put them in debt, I'd made their lives a misery and whenever they'd trusted me I'd screwed them. But we all said we'd try again.

They did and I didn't. I couldn't stop using, and I needed money. When I met a girl I'd known in treatment we decided to go on the streets as a double act. She had a car, and I knew the business. We started to work the area behind the Cumberland Hotel, doing tricks in the back of the car, anything with anyone. Ugly, weird nights with the kind of men who look respectable but aren't. I often wondered where they got their money. They paid well.

One night I made two or three hundred pounds, scored, and went home. I didn't even want to have a fix. Couldn't have made it anyway,

I was sobbing too hard to find a vein, sitting on the bed surrounded by drugs, hating them, hating myself, hating life. Useless. And yet I knew other addicts had been through everything I'd been through and beaten it. I wasn't unique. After years of thinking I was a special case, I had to admit that I was just another junkie, a typical, boring junkie.

We had another family meeting. My parents thought that now they knew about my addiction it might be easier to help, but I don't think they realised how bad it was going to be, listening to the same hopeless stuff over and over and over again. I could see it was killing my father, I could see it in his face – too much for me to cope with, so I went into the toilet next door and fixed up, about ten feet away from where he was trying not to crack. Always trust a junkie to let you down.

*   *   *

I had another overdose, my third. The first thing I did when I came round was to reach for the syringe. Part of me knew that one day I wouldn't come round, and part of me didn't care. AIDS from an infected needle, or a terminal overdose, what was the difference? It was madness. I was going mad, there was no other explanation that I could think of, and I decided that it would be best if I was locked away. I asked my mother to have me committed to a mental hospital.

She refused. She said I was sick, not mad.

She'd do anything else for me, but she wouldn't stick me in an asylum.

So I left, found a private mental hospital and committed myself. Paid for the room in advance, met the male nurse who was going to put me in a straightjacket if I got violent, gave him anything I might use to commit suicide, put on the regulation white cotton shift and stared at the wall. At night I stared at the ceiling. Sleep was impossible because of the screams coming from the other rooms. I longed for a hit.

After a week, I had to get out, and I left on my twenty-fourth birthday. If I kept on using, and if the policeman had been right about what he'd told me, I had one year to go. Fuck it. I went out and scored, but it didn't help the way it used to, didn't put my mind out completely. Some tiny, stubborn part of my brain refused to switch off, and it kept forcing me to look at myself – weak, stupid, selfish and totally futile.

My parents had taken all they could take. They knew I was killing myself, day by day, and they couldn't bear the thought of having to sit there and watch it happen, of going into my room one morning and finding me dead in bed with a needle hanging from my arm.

So they gave me an ultimatum: if you're going to keep on using, you're not going to do it in front of us. Go away, leave the house and don't ever come back. Ever. But if you're really going to try to stop, if you accept that you can't do it on your own, if you accept help, then we'll always

74

be here for you. That's the choice, and you have to make it. We can't.

They meant it. They said it all very quietly, and I think that shocked me more than shouting or tears or anger. They'd made up their minds to shut the door on me if I went on using. For the first time in my life I wouldn't have them to run back to, the safety net I'd always counted on wouldn't be there, the only people in the world I now trusted would be out if I came to call. It finally sunk in that I'd used up all my credit.

*   *   *

My cousin in Italy was pregnant, and my mother wanted to go and see her. She took me, although she knew I was on pills to help me off smack, and then she told the family in Italy that I was an addict. There was no sympathy from them. My cousin, my friend from childhood, looked at me as though I was infectious. She patted her belly, and told me I'd never see the baby if I kept on using. She didn't want someone like me anywhere near her children. She didn't want them catching my disease.

First my parents, now my relatives. There would be no more family if I stayed on drugs. Nobody. It was the last straw. I went to my room, took the pills from where I'd hidden them, flushed them down the toilet and waited for panic to set in.

All the books I'd read about coming off drugs had told me what to expect, physically and

75

emotionally, and I'd been through it before, more than once. But there's another problem, a simple practical problem: what do you do instead of getting stoned? For years, I'd spent most of every day hustling and scoring and fixing. Being a junkie takes up twenty-four hours a day, and that's a lot of time to fill when it suddenly stretches ahead of you, empty. Since the age of twelve, drugs had been my life. What the hell did straight people do with their lives? Work and friends, hobbies and interests? I had none of those, and each day was a long, blank tunnel.

Funnily enough, I was helped by windsurfing, which I'd never thought of as a substitute for methadone. Windsurfing looked easy when other people did it, but I kept falling off. Each time I fell I became more determined to get the hang of it. And one day there must have been a kind wind blowing, because I got up and stayed up.

I stood on the board, my mouth clean with the taste of salt water, the sun in my face and the wind on my back, hearing the slap-slap of the waves as the board went faster and faster. I found that I could change direction without falling off, I could control where I was going. My body was working and the air seemed to shine. Speed and control – the feeling reminded me of something and I couldn't understand it. I was high without dope.

It didn't last long, just a few minutes, but they were fantastic minutes, my first experience of being happy and straight at the same time, one tiny taste of a different kind of life. It was enough to make me want more, and I told my mother I was going to try – really try – to come off drugs and stay off. If it didn't work, I'd leave home and get on with dying by myself.

Saying it in Italy was a lot easier than sticking to it in London. My parents thought I could do it, Joyce Ditzler thought I could do it, and other addicts at NA meetings told me I could do it. But I'd failed before, so often, and I kept seeing users and dealers I knew with pockets full of gear. One hit wouldn't hurt. Straight days were so long. I could feel my willpower melting.

Joyce knew, and she knew that if I stayed in London I wouldn't last. Too many old contacts, too easy to score, the alcoholic let loose in a brewery. She told me I had to find something to do instead of drifting through the days and paying lip service at NA meetings, I had to do it a long way from London, ideally in another country. But do what? All I'd learned in twelve years was to hustle and be handy with a needle. I had no faith in my ability to boil an egg, let alone use my brain. That had been out of action for half my life.

Joyce must have felt like hitting me. Everyone was trying to help, and I was looking for reasons why nothing would work. I was used to failure and defeat, and I wasn't going to give them up without a struggle. They were habits too.

It was my luck that other people didn't give up as quickly as me. My parents and Joyce agreed to send me away to school to learn French, and they chose a small town in Switzerland – quiet, clean Switzerland, where people work hard and go to bed early. It's difficult to imagine a Swiss junkie, it doesn't fit in with the national character. Maybe that was one of the reasons for picking Lausanne.

Another trip to the bank for my father, another loan, and then a month of waiting before the beginning of term. I was looking forward to it and dreading it – being on my own with straight people, having to concentrate and work and stay clean all at once. I couldn't do it. I was sure I couldn't do it. Shit. I went out and scored. Felt guilty and worthless. Scored again. Oh God, here we go. One more week of this and the school would have one less student.

The months of treatment and going to NA meetings and the hours with Joyce might not have convinced me that I could come off drugs. I was still trying to compromise and do it my own way. But at least I'd learned to ask for help. Once again I went to my parents and once again they held me up. My mother didn't give me any advice. She just told me to pack. The school term wasn't starting for a few days, but we'd go by train to Switzerland, the longest way round. And we'd go the next day. Pack.

I had a stash in my room, no smack but enough pills to keep me stoned all the way to Switzerland, and I knew I should leave them behind. And I knew I wouldn't. They went into my bag, a hand-

78

ful of insurance in case the train started closing in on me. I wouldn't use them unless I had to, the same old song.

All the way from London to Paris I stared at the bag where I'd hidden the pills. I don't know whether I was more scared of them or of going to school. If I took them I'd be off again, and I knew how that would end. Did I want to live or did I want to die?

The train arrived in Paris, and we had to take the Metro to the hotel. There was rubbish bin on the platform. I took the pills and threw them away. I felt as though I'd jumped out of a plane without a parachute.

7

STAYING CLEAN

'If you start using again, you're coming back to England and you're going back into treatment.'

My mother hugged me and wished me luck. I'm sure she kept her fingers crossed all the way home to London.

I was a twenty-four-year-old student who had never learned how to study, the product of a short, stoned education. What was I supposed to do with these empty notebooks? There were other students saying in the hostel, and I asked one of them to tell me what I should do. He looked at me as though I'd just arrived from Mars. He was Spanish; he probably thought that English girls spent their school years playing cricket.

School was a mental assault course. We started at eight, had lessons until one, two hours' revision, more lessons, tests every week. My head hurt from the exercise my brain was getting and going to bed with a headache was part of the daily routine – almost an enjoyable part, because it made me feel as though I'd done something. I was nervous about taking pain-killers, even ordinary aspirin. Pills frightened me.

A strange thing happened, the first time addiction had ever worked for me. I found myself getting hooked on studying. Knowledge and learning fascinated me. I wanted to cram a year's course into three months, and then to go on until I was good enough not just to speak French, but to teach it. I wanted to score in the classroom. It was a normal, straight ambition, but I felt I'd made an amazing discovery, somewhere else to put all the energy that used to go into hustling. After years of starvation, my brain was being fed. I passed my first exams.

It was a shock, too good to be true, so I couldn't believe that it was the result of the work I'd put in. I had it fixed in my mind that junkies and ex-junkies were mental cripples, not the kind of people who pass exams. I hadn't turned into Einstein overnight, I was still the same worthless dummy. I'd just been lucky. I couldn't accept that I'd changed enough to achieve anything.

But although part of my head was still stuck in the past, the rest of me was adapting to being clean, sometimes not in the way I'd hoped. Not for the first time, my hair started falling out and I put on weight like a Christmas turkey. I could still feel the after-effects of drugs, attacks of shivering or twitching as though ghosts were passing through my body.

81

Withdrawal often has exactly the opposite effect of the drug. If you come off speed you feel depressed and slow, if you come off downers you feel wired and agitated, and if you come off the mixture that I'd been pumping into myself you feel as though all your sensations have been shaken up together in a bag and then emptied out inside you. I never knew what to expect. My moods came and went: violence, calmness, optimism, depression – the only constant feeling was the urge to soak up more knowledge, to get another fix from another book.

There was one slip. It was the night before an exam, harder and more important than the others I thought I'd been lucky to pass, and I was talking myself into failing.

And so I went out and scored – even in Lausanne you could score – and snorted some smack. It was the same wonderful hit it had always been, and it scared me rigid. All the memories came back with the high, the memories of dirt and despair and emptiness, the useless days and the ugly nights. That's what life would be if I did any more heroin, and I knew it. I finally recognised I was making progress.

But the pull was still there, very close, and I don't think I would have made it without NA. Nothing helps me as much as talking to other addicts. They know, in a way that straight people can't know, what it's like to look over the edge and be tempted to jump. How easy it is to kid yourself that you can have just the one hit.

I had a sponsor at AA who pulled me through more than once. Anne was patient and tough, a sympathetic bully. She refused to let me let her down, and if there were medals for sponsors she'd be clanking with them.

Help came in other ways. My hair grew back and I lost weight, so I was saved from being the only bald, fat girl in the class. I passed more exams, and had to cope with the new feeling that I might not be a moron after all. It wasn't quite self-respect, but it was a start. And every six or eight weeks, when my mother came out to see me, the pleasure she got from seeing me straight gave me pleasure as well. I was learning.

I had the chance to move out of the student hostel and into a tiny apartment with another girl, and I celebrated by throwing away the one last secret joint I'd kept like a security blanket: totally clean for the first time in twelve years.

And almost totally useless around the apartment, since my domestic abilities began and ended with making my bed. As far as shopping, paying bills, cooking and housework were concerned I was twelve years old, and my girlfriend couldn't understand it. Where had I been when I should have been growing up? I had to tell her, and I found it was no worse than admitting that I'd been very ill. I was amazed. I could talk to a straight person about drugs, and I wasn't treated like a walking disease.

Every day I discovered feelings that the straight world takes for granted. Waking up healthy – not shivering, not craving a hit – was new. The smell of coffee, the taste of a fresh croissant, clean hair, clean sheets, a clean head – all the fuzz was dropping away, and my feelings were coming back into sharp focus. Everything was new. Even feeling hungry was new; not the hunger of an empty stomach needing fuel, but the hunger for flavours and textures.

I remember the first time I ate oysters, and how I loved the slippery taste of the sea. An hour or so later there was a riot in my stomach, another strange new feeling. Was this what oysters did? It wasn't until I'd thrown up that I realised I'd eaten a bad one.

I had to change my mind about straight people after half a lifetime of treating them like the enemy. I'd looked down on them before, when I'd started on drugs, because they didn't know what I knew, didn't get high like I did. That changed to envy when drugs took over my life and I could see that straight people had something I wanted, and I hated them for it. Now I was straight, even though I was only a beginner and there were lessons to be learned before I could qualify as normal. Twelve years was a lot to catch up.

I felt old and young at the same time. Other students seemed very innocent, twenty years younger than me, when they talked about their lives. And yet when I had my first straight boyfriend I could have been fifteen, shy and nervous and not knowing what to do. Holding hands was a big event, a physical tingle. Queensway and the crawlers were a million years away in a different, numb life. I wasn't numb any more.

And very gradually, I came to believe what I'd been told so many times by so many people: addicts aren't bad people trying to be good, but sick people who need help to get better. It's obvious and it's true and I'd resisted it for years. As long as I'd resisted it I'd always gone back to using, and then I could say that I'd been right about myself, useless and incurable.

It's hard to get out of that way of thinking – for me, harder than it had been to stop using. That was only the first stage, and it was simple; not easy, but simple. Clearing out the mess from the body can be measured in months. Clearing out the mess in the head can take years, and I had to grow a new set of emotions from scratch. I'd never trusted myself – I'd had plenty of reasons not to – I had no self-respect, no confidence in my ability to do anything normal, no real hope that the future would be any better than the past.

Asking for help was painful, because it made me feel vulnerable. Believing anything good was a major effort. I'd been a champion at self-destruction, always ready to snatch defeat from the jaws of victory, and to change a basic attitude like that is a slow trip up a steep hill.

There were days when the most ordinary moments were magical. I remember sitting on the tiny terrace of my tiny apartment having breakfast, watching the light on the lake and the mountains, listening to music, feeling healthy, looking forward to a day at school, half-thinking I was going to wake up and find myself in the squat and then realising I wasn't. It was better than the best high. I'd been told that coming off drugs could be an adventure, and that I could have the kind of life I never dreamed I could have. I'd put it down as bullshit, and I was wrong. This was it. I was on the other side of the window I'd been looking though for years.

But even today, I can't take normal life for granted. I still feel as if I've just learned to swim and been thrown into the sea – the thrill of staying afloat is there, but so is the fear of sinking. And little, ordinary things can be a problem. Like everyone, I get depressed. I used to get high to shake it off. Now I have to work it out by myself, without the pills and needles. Meeting new people and making new friends is never the simple, pleasant experience it should be. Will they like me once they know what I was and what I did? How *could* they like me? It's hard to stop thinking of myself as worthless, hard to admit to other people that I was a junkie, and probably hard for some of them to accept. I know that addiction is a disease, but do they? Every time I tell the truth about the past to someone new, I half-expect to be rejected.

There are other days, dangerous days, when I think I've won and I've learned enough to control drugs. Maybe I could have a smoke, maybe a snort. Maybe I could take it or leave it, 'occasional use for pleasure'. Maybe I'm not an addict any more. I remember how good it had been at the beginning. And then, with my new, honest memory, I remember how bad it had been at the end.

The fact is that addicts are always addicts. The lucky ones recover, and with understanding and help more and more of them will recover. But there's no such thing as a personality transplant. The bug is still there, and all you can do to stop it from turning into a monster is to starve it. There is no permanent, absolute cure. There is only the daily cure, and there are times when even twenty-four hours are too much to get through alone. I still go to NA meetings and spend hours talking to people like Joyce and Anne who held me up when I was ready to give in.

Work helps too, and I chase business as hard as I used to chase junk. Dealing with businessmen is not all that different from dealing with junkies. Everyone wants to score one way or another, and a man in a suit can be just as flaky as a smack dealer in a squat. I wouldn't recommend dealing dope as training for a business career, but it taught me something about human nature, so perhaps it wasn't all wasted.

The biggest waste, and a sadness that will never go away, is the lost time with my mother and father. I can never make up for what I did to them, and I can never repay them for what they did for me. We're very close now, probably closer than most families. I can't think of anyone of my age whose best friends are their parents, and I'd do anything to give them back what I took away. I know that's impossible.

I've been clean now for five years, but the past is as close as a shadow. Drugs took everything and gave back nothing, and I try to remember that whenever the old bad feeling of wanting a hit comes back. It still happens, and I expect it always will. But for today I'm a recovered addict, today is another gift, today I have what I never had when I was using – I can choose how to live, and choice is freedom. When I was using I couldn't choose. In the end, the memory of that is more likely to keep me straight than anything else.

This story is only what happened to me, one case out of hundreds of thousands. I wanted to tell it because I couldn't believe how little most people know about such a huge and terrible problem, and how much less they know about the solution.

And there *is* a solution. It's slow and difficult, but it works. There are thousands of addicts like me, in recovery, to prove that it works. Sometimes the support and strength they get from NA is enough. Sometimes they need treatment as well. But as long as there's life there's hope of recovery. No addict, however down and desperate, is beyond help.

It can be done. It worked for me. Life is sweet.